INSIDE
AMARC

INSIDE
AMARC

The
Aerospace Maintenance and Regeneration Center
Tucson, Arizona

JERRY FUGERE
and
BOB SHANE - Photographer

Airlife
England

Copyright Photographs © 2001 Bob Shane

First published in the UK in 2001
by Airlife Publishing Ltd

British Library Cataloguing-in-Publication Data
  A catalogue record for this book
  is available from the British Library

ISBN 1 84037 117 X

Typeset by Celtic, Wrexham
Printed in Singapore by Kyodo Printing Co. (S'pore) Pte Ltd.

Airlife Publishing Ltd
101 Longden Road, Shrewsbury, SY3 9EB, England
E-mail: airlife@airlifebooks.com
Website: www.airlifebooks.com

ACKNOWLEDGEMENTS

This book, a complete guide to AMARC's Phantom Air Force, is not only about aircraft, it is about people and the processes under which they operate; it's about the pilots that bring the aircraft in, the personnel that meet the aircraft as they arrive and the people that maintain them while they are in storage. Every person that has brought an aircraft into AMARC has something to do with this book. Every person that has been or is presently employed at AMARC has in some way been intimately involved with the publication of this book. It depicts what AMARC is: A Storage Facility that Maintains and Regenerates Aircraft. Each photo was specifically selected to depict a part of the operation as it occurs. Special thanks go to the pilots that flew their aircraft in, not knowing what the final disposition of the aircraft would be; whether it would go to a foreign country, to another government agency, be used as a drone to be shot down ultimately by air-to-air missiles or cut up in accordance with the Strategic Arms Reduction Treaty. Special thanks go out to the crew chiefs and ground crews that were so dedicated to their aircraft while they were in operational status to complete their missions and bring their aircrews safely home. Nothing is more rewarding than to hear the wheels touch down after a long, successful mission. Lastly, the author wishes to express his personal thanks for having had the opportunity to be a part of this highly professional AMARC organization.

CONTENTS

INTRODUCTION

Many years ago it was determined that Tucson was an ideal location for the storage of aircraft. The relatively low rainfall, the low humidity and the caliche base for parking aircraft, were all determining factors. Utilizing the runway at Davis-Monthan Air Force Base, the aircraft could taxi right up to the receiving line where the pilot could sign the aircraft over to AMARC, thus starting a process that could retain an aircraft in storage in a combat ready, flyable configuration for many years. The technical data used for the preservation would be generic for all aircraft.

This premier storage facility is known as The Aerospace Maintenance and Regeneration Center (AMARC). It is the single Department of Defense facility for the storage of all Army, Navy, Air Force and Coast Guard aircraft. AMARC encompasses 2,712 acres with thirteen miles of perimeter fenceline. At the present time there are approximately 5,000 aircraft in storage with an acquisition value of eighteen billion dollars. The big influx at the end of the Cold War accounted for the arrival of the more sophisticated aircraft; the F-14, F-15, F-111, and the KC-135. Although the primary mission of AMARC is to remove parts from aircraft and return then to the active inventory, there are many other responsibilities that are assumed as overseers of these important assets. Careful consideration must be given to each aircraft as it arrives. Each aircraft, or weapon system, is owned by a System Program Manager who will select which type of storage the aircraft will go into upon arrival at AMARC. Upon arrival, the process will commence using technical data that is generic to all aircraft in that particular type of storage. The types of storage are: Type 1000 storage which pertains to aircraft that will ultimately be flown again; Type 2000 storage for those aircraft that have been selected as parts donors; Type 3000 storage for aircraft in temporary storage selected to fly out in the next 90 to 180 days; and Type 4000 storage for aircraft considered excess to the inventory and destined to be turned into Defense Reutilization and Marketing Office (DRMO) for final disposition.

The Processes of
Receiving, Preserving,
Reclamation and
Disposition

In 1997, AMARC celebrated its 50th Anniversary. For those who can remember that far back, the facility was originally established to store those aircraft returning from World War II. Since they were no longer required, there would be parts removed and ultimately, the aircraft would be chopped up and melted down into aluminum ingots. That philosophy continued through the years until the Air Force was designated as the single manager for aerospace assets in storage. Along with that decision came the renaming of the organization to the Military Aircraft Storage and Disposition Center (MASDC) and the responsibility for the storage of all aircraft from all military services.

Then came the Vietnam Conflict and the need to induct some of these stored aircraft back into operational use. During that era there were 625 aircraft and more than 259,000 parts returned to the active inventory. Then came the end to that conflict so all those aircraft were processed back into storage and by the end of 1973 there were a total of 6,080 in storage.

Then, in 1985, the organization was renamed again; this time to The Aerospace Maintenance and Regeneration Center (AMARC), realizing that we were not a Boneyard or a Graveyard but a storage facility that maintained and regenerated aircraft. That's where this story begins.

The reorganization was established utilizing three processes: Process-In, Process-Out and Reclamation. Process-In consisted of meeting the aircraft and having the aircraft signed over to AMARC. The aircraft was made safe by removing the Cad/Pad items (items required for seat and canopy ejection). An Examination and Evaluation (E&E) was then commenced, making a complete inventory of all the items assigned to that aircraft. Once that was completed the aircraft was towed to the Flush Farm where all the fuel was drained and stored for future use and the aircraft was filled to capacity with 10/10 oil, which was our preservative. The engines were motored to preserve the moving parts within and preserve the fuel system. Then they were taken to the Corrosion Control facility (wash rack) where the wheel bearings were greased, the aircraft lubricated, corrosion was treated and arrested and the aircraft was washed in preparation for the third step of the storage process, the spraylat process. There are also three steps to the spraylat process, covering all the production breaks with tape, spraying the areas with a black, elastic waterproof latex paint called Spraylat, and then covering that area with a white material of the same texture and consistency called Kool-Kote, a material that will reflect the sun, allowing for a ten to fifteen degree variance with the outside temperature. Although this procedure was used on all storage processes, those aircraft in Type 1000 storage would be represerved at the end of four years, reversing the storage process by taking them in from the field, removing the spraylat, washing the aircraft, taking it to the Flush Farm, filling it with fuel, running the engines and all systems as if they were preparing the aircraft for flight, and then reversing the storage process again to put it back into storage for another four years. Type 2000 program storage would be for aircraft that would be selected as parts donors in the future; however, the preservation process would be the same as Type 1000 storage except for lubricating the aircraft. Type 3000 program storage would be for those aircraft that would be turned around in 90–180 days for flyaway, running the engines every forty-five days; and Type 4000 program storage would include those aircraft that have no future use and would ultimately be turned in to Defense Reutilization and Marketing office (DRMO) for resale to the public.

Process-Out would remove the aircraft from the field and prepare them for flyaway. The Drone aircraft are included in this category. The aircraft would be taken to the wash rack where the spraylat would be removed, the aircraft washed, the engine(s) would be removed and sent to the engine shop where a thorough inspection would be accomplished while the aircraft was being disassembled and inspected. All the removable parts would be thoroughly inspected, bench checked and later reinstalled. The aircraft would undergo a complete overhaul before being readied for flight. The engine(s) would be trimmed out in the Engine Test Cell and when determined to be fully operational would be reinstalled in the aircraft and tested again before being released for flight. The test pilot would flight test the aircraft, release it for flight and deliver the aircraft to the contractor, who would install the remote control equipment and deliver the aircraft to Tyndall AFB, Florida, where it would be flown for fifty hours as a remote control, ground operated, air-to-air simulator for air-to-air combat for the young pilots of today. At the end of fifty hours they would be shot down by the 'aggressor' pilot. Many other aircraft are prepared for flight; Foreign Military Sales aircraft, State Department for the Drug Interdiction program, NASA, and other government organizations. Process-Out has been responsible for launching out 152 F-102s, 312 F-100s, 156 F-106s and are presently involved with preparing 354 F-4E/G/RFs as Drone aircraft. No major accidents have occurred since the Drone Program was initiated.

The Reclamation Process is the driving force of AMARC. The process starts when the Reclamation supply clerks receive requests from the Item Manager who receives a demand from the operational units. A copy of the request is given to the Reclamation planners who research the requested part in the respective technical data to ascertain the exact location of the part on the aircraft, determine the possible interchangeables, and provide this package to the Reclamation Priority Removal crews. A priority removal notice will accompany the technical data that allows the crews to go to those aircraft that have that particular item on board. Once the part is removed it is inspected for serviceability, the item checked operationally, if required, and prepared for shipment to the operational unit. Fiscal year 1997 proved very profitable to the Air Force with 21,207 parts reclaimed back into the active inventory, 454 aircraft processed in and 251 aircraft processed out, for a total savings of $861 million dollars. Operating on a fifty-one million dollar budget, for every dollar spent AMARC had a return of seventeen dollars. The Reclamation Division is also responsible for the removal of parts included in the routine reclamation save lists that are generated by the System Program Managers, involving the removal of all serviceable, repairable assets from the aircraft and sending them to the Depot for repair prior to making them available to the operational units. The Reclamation Division also prepares aircraft for overland transportation to meet customers' needs as static displays, special projects, or for Foreign Military Sales. Aircraft that are no longer capable of flying are prepared as ground targets in the gunnery ranges and shipped overland by the Reclamation crews. Every part in AMARC is considered a viable asset until determined otherwise by the System Program Manager, who will direct AMARC to turn the part into DRMO to be sold to the civilian market.

△ This four-wheel drive security police vehicle is one driven by Sgt J.J. Guajado, one of the many elite security policemen assigned to patrol the 2,712 acres, thirteen miles of fenceline that surround AMARC. These elite airmen patrol the perimeter of AMARC twenty-four hours a day and provide security at the two entry points.

Following Page: As you enter the AMARC facility from the Kolb and Irvington Roads you will be greeted by this wonderful desert scene. It signifies the single Department of Defense (DOD) facility for the storage of aircraft, managed by the Air Force Materiel Command.

▲ Once the aircraft are received, they are towed to this ramp where the seats and canopy explosive devises (Cad/Pads) are removed, the E&E is accomplished and they stand ready to begin the Process-In. The temporary parking area is AM-2 matting; aluminum matting that is matched together. Hopefully, in the future, the matting will be replaced with concrete.

▼ Looking from the south at 11,000 ft, one can see the approximately 5,000 aircraft stored at AMARC. Most distinguishable are the 284 B-52s located in the START area where 347 B-52s will be cut up in accordance with the Treaty. This is where it all happens: aircraft arriving for permanent storage; parts being removed and returned to the active inventory; aircraft being prepared for flyaway as drones; Forestry Service waterdroppers; Drug Interdiction aircraft for South America; aircraft to hunt down poachers in Africa; C-130s for Equador, Oman and Argentina; P-3As for Chile; AT-38s for Taiwan pilot training at Holloman AFB, NM; OV-10s for the Latin American Air Force Academy at Lackland AFB, TX; static displays for the museums as well as the museum trade planes. Always preparing aircraft for materials testing by the Wright Laboratories from Wright-Patterson AFB, OH. Only 720 people to do all this work!! They are hard to find when they are spread over the 2,712 acres. Fiscal year 92 reported 157 aircraft back into the active inventory, 33,102 parts returned to the active inventory for a total of $680 million. Operating on a budget of $36.5 million, for every dollar spent $18.64 was returned. Total assets: 12.175 billion dollars of acquisition value (the purchase price of the aircraft when new).

This F-4G was the 1,000th F-4 assigned to AMARC. The aircraft was piloted by Capt. Charles Smith of the 561st FS, George AFB, CA. Although many F-4s were assigned to AMARC, this F-4 accounted for the 1,000th on station at the time of arrival. This aircraft may well be selected to fly back out for the Drone program.

On 11 May 93 the first C-141B arrived for Process-In into AMARC. C-141B 66-0143 arrived from the 97th AMW, Altus AFB, OK. Piloted by Capt. Todd Anderson, Co-pilot Capt. Henry Steenken, Flight Engineers SMSgt Robert Myers and SSgt Bruce Taft. 0143 had a total of 31,600.4 flight hours terminating at Davis-Monthan AFB, AZ.

B-52G 59-2589 arrived on 17 June 92 from Barksdale AFB, LA, after completing 15,095 flying hours. Note the nose art that was painted over, indicating participation in Operation Desert Storm where much beautiful nose art depicting female gender had to be painted over to please the government of Saudi Arabia. This B-52G was also the winner of the Fairchild Trophy, awarded to the winner of the Strategic Air Command Bombing Competition. It also proudly bears the insignia of the Master Crew Chief, representing SAC's finest of Maintenance Technicians.

PAGES 16 & 17: Aerial view of the Receiving ramp, Flush Farm and Shelter work area. 3/95

This B-52G was the last B-52G to arrive at AMARC from Barksdale AFB, LA, as part of the START (21 Dec. 92). The Aircraft Commander, B/Gen. Cole, was met by his father, B/Gen. Cole (Ret.). The other members of the crew were Lt Col Spears, Maj. Langford, and SSgt Debbie Walke, Barksdale AFB, LA.

▲ These are the Boys from Sioux City, Iowa. On 20 Feb. 92, a flight of
A-7Ds arrived from the Iowa Air National Guard, Sioux City, Iowa,
celebrating the last flight of one of the pilots who was retiring after
twenty-six years. Of course, as tradition might have it, that called for a
water washdown and a bottle of champagne, provided by the author,
Jerry Fugere.

▼ This Navy F-14A is going through the preservation process by
spraying 10/10 oil into the engine intakes, allowing the oil to
penetrate the internal parts of the engine. All systems will be operated
during this process.

▲ This HH-53 Sea Stallion is awaiting Process-In.

▼ September 1979 saw the end to the competition between the Boeing YC-14 and the McDonnell Douglas YC-15. Here the YC-15 is having its JT-8D-17 engines removed and returned to McDonnell Douglas. The induction into AMARC ended a seven-year competition that started in 1972 when the Air Force called for a medium/heavy short field take off and landing (STOL) transport that would last into the next century. The YC-15 introduced in this aircraft four engines that would produce 64,000 lb of thrust and have a cargo area of 6,214 sq. ft. The effect of the exhaust from the engines blowing across the lower surface of the wings and down the flaps with a maximum angle of fifty-two degrees allowed for ultimate STOL capabilities. The YC-15 is completely computerized for on-load, off-load, weight and balance, with the cockpit designed from the DC-10.

▲ B-52G 59-2579 having its turn on the Flush Farm. Although the later arrival B-52Gs are being processed into storage under Type 4000, the process has been modified to include the preservation of the fuel systems and engines for future use, prior to being cut up in accordance with START.

◀ Flush Farm. 7/94

▼ Prior to the aircraft going to the Flush Farm, it will undergo an Examination and Evaluation (E&E), making a complete inventory of the aircraft, removing classified items, recording all serial numbers of high value equipment and documenting the type systems that are in the aircraft. This A-7D has its wings folded to save parking space.

▲ This membrane building was built to accommodate the analytical condition inspection (ACI) on the OA-37A aircraft; however, the project was picked up by San Antonio ALC, so now it is used to prepare aircraft for flight, such as this F-4, as well as de-arm the squibs for the jettison system on the F-111A capsules.

▼ The TA-4J is undergoing a part of the corrosion control process, the second step of the Process-In that every aircraft will experience before being placed in storage. An in-depth inspection to treat and arrest any corrosion, greasing the wheel bearings, lubricating the aircraft, and a thorough wash job will be accomplished prior to going to the spraylat process.

▲ Removing the Martin-Baker seats from this F-4E from Clark AB, Philippines, in the heat of summer at AMARC can be a tedious task. Here a T-33 canopy cover is used to block the sun as the Cad/Pad (explosive devises) items are removed prior to removing the seat. The F-4E rests on the AM-2 matting.

▼ The production breaks on the F-16A are taped prior to spraylatting.

▲ The intakes and exhausts are covered with heavy duty aluminum foil or barrier paper and then sprayed with spraylat and Kool-Kote.

◄ Early 1992 saw the arrival of the first EC-135s in AMARC, ending a thirty-five year career as Airborne Command Posts (Looking Glass). 55-3129 was assigned to Langley AFB, VA. Here the preservation process continues as the radome is being spraylatted. These former airborne command posts were not destined to fly again and were placed in Type 2000 storage, allowing parts to be removed to support the active fleet.

▼ This F-4E has just completed the spraylat process and, using a little ingenuity, the spraylat technician saves the shark-mouth that made the squadron at Clark AB, Philippines famous during the war in Vietnam. The aircraft could be included with the other F-4Es as air-to-air combat simulators (Drones).

▲ A-10A 77-0266 arrived at AMARC on 26 Oct. 92 from the 926 Ftr Gp, 706 Ftr Sq, NAS New Orleans, LA. The black elastic waterproof latex material (Spraylat) has been applied. Next the Kool-Kote will be applied to reflect the sun, allowing for a ten to fifteen degree variance with the outside temperature.

▶ The more than 200 Navy F-4N/Ss are stored at AMARC in plasticized canvas bags which the Navy has determined more economically feasible, rather than utilizing the spraylat process. The bag can be easily rolled back to allow the removal of parts from the cockpit without having to reseal the spraylat. The bag offers considerable savings, being good for a period of eight years in storage which would require two spraylat represervation cycles.

▼ This KA-6D rests on Display Row displaying a unique canvas bag that was used as a PRAM (Productivity/ Reliability/Availability/ Maintainability) project to determine the economical feasibility of using the bag in lieu of the spraylat.

▲ Prior to a large influx of aircraft arriving at AMARC, a parking plan has to be established. To properly park the aircraft in straight rows and plan on a maximum number of aircraft in a confined area, the area is surveyed with this surveyor's tripod and stakes are driven in the ground to mark the spot for the nose gear.

▶ The Process-Out ramp displays various types of aircraft preparing to depart the storage facility. 3/94

▼ This nose to tail parking plan is common with the P-3A/Bs as with all the aircraft parked in storage at AMARC, to allow for the maximum amount of aircraft in a confined area. The protruding tails of the P-3A/Bs house magnetic tracking devices that were primarily used to track submarines during the Cold War.

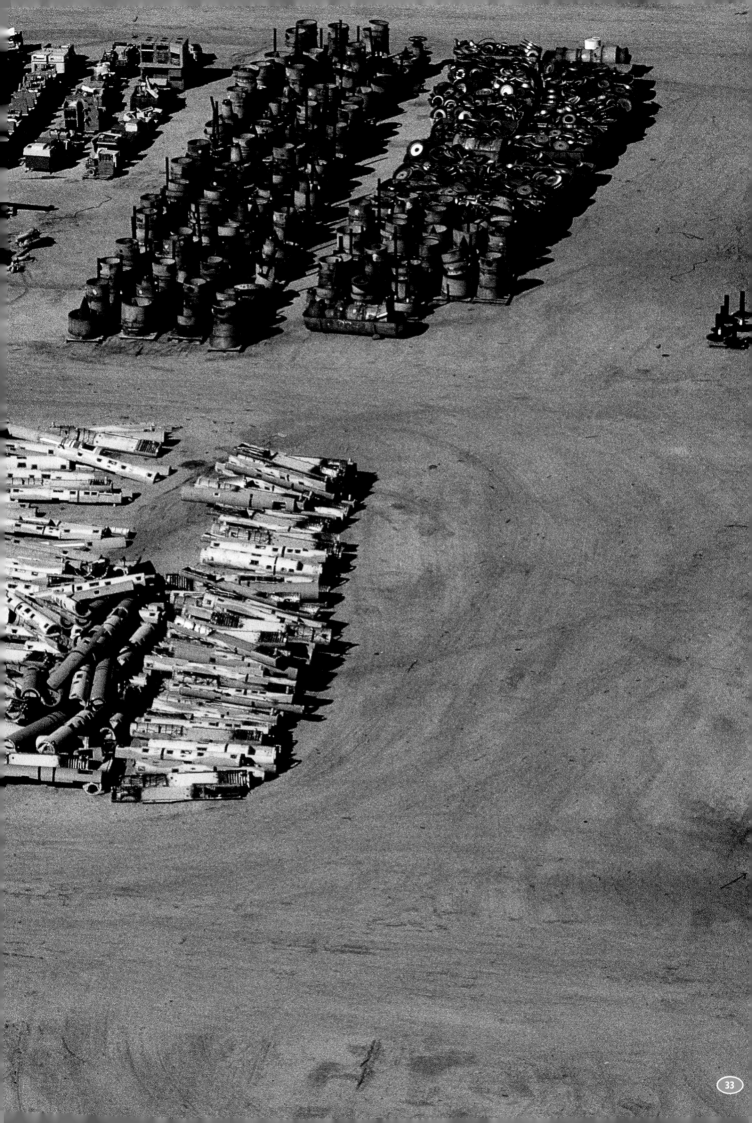

Pages 32 & 33: This scrap heap in DRMO represents the 445 Ground Launch Cruise Missiles that were brought to AMARC to be cut in half in accordance with the INF Treaty. Prior to the cut there were twenty-seven line items removed and returned to the Navy inventory. They were stockpiled until the Soviets could identify them by serial number and then they were cut in half, very closely monitored by the Soviets.

This American Trans Air 707-300 has had all its essential parts removed and was one of the first 707s sold through DRMO to Southwest Alloy, a contractor located to the east of AMARC that chopped up the aircraft and melted it down into aluminum ingots. Southwest Alloy purchased the first sixty-three 707s declared excess and sold through DRMO.

Among the many predators roaming the 2,712 acres of AMARC is the giant Gila Monster. It was rather unusual catching him in the full scope of sunlight as he is usually found hiding in the shade.

II
Aircraft in Storage

IIA CELEBRITY ROW

▼ As one enters the AMARC from the Wilmot gate and passes the AMARC sign, one will review the aircraft on Celebrity Row, a display representing a portion of the aircraft that we have on the facility. Most conspicuous is the Super Guppy, a NASA aircraft built from a KC-97J that departed AMARC in 1965, to carry the Saturn IV and V Boosters and the Lunar Module. The aircraft on display represent trainers, fighters, bombers, cargo, experimental, museum assets, and, of course, the ACET vehicle used to transport F-4s out of the field in the event of a contingency during the rainy or monsoon season.

▶ 'Display Row' otherwise known as 'Celebrity Row' represents a portion of the aircraft that we have in the facility. There are more than eighty-four different types of aircraft in storage.

▲ B-57E next to a WB-57.

▼ This C-22A was operating in Panama prior to its arrival in AMARC. The aircraft has significant corrosion damage and will be used for parts to support the other C-22s in the system.

▲ One of the newest aircraft to arrive at AMARC, the C-27A Rapid Response Intra-Theater Airlifter operated by the Southern Area Command in Panama by the 310th Airlift Sq. Landing on austere (unpaved) runways of 1,800 ft, the C-27A can carry thirty-four Troops, or up to a maximum of 19,861 lb of cargo. The first C-27A was delivered on 20 Aug. 91. Although only ten C-27As operated in Panama, a total of ninety-five serve elsewhere around the world.

▼ This Boeing YC-14A, painted in the camouflage color scheme, rolled off the production line on 9 Aug. 76. Both Boeing prototypes exceeded their projected delivery dates and were flown on 369 sorties for a total of 601.31 hours by eighty-one different pilots.

▲ This ACET vehicle or more specifically named the Air Cushioned Equipment Transporter is used in the event of a contingency during the monsoons when we are called upon to generate F-4s. The operator would sit in the front and winch the F-4 on to the vehicle. He would fire up the two turbine engines in the front, which would in turn, lift the whole unit a foot off the ground, thus operating as a hydroplane. A tractor would tow it to the Shelter where crews would download and generate the F-4.

▲ The F-101C was a popular aircraft for static display. Although many would be processed through Reclamation, returning the viable assets to the active inventory, many would be fortunate enough to be selected as static display aircraft.

▼ These F-102s are museum assets for static display, the one on top being a TF-102, a side by side trainer that was used to train B-58 pilots.

This F-105G 'Wild Weasel' was very instrumental in attacking SAM missile sites in Vietnam. The aircraft is now a prime candidate for static display under the Air Force Museum Program.

Aerial F-111s. 2/94

Here at the foot of the Santa Catalina Mountains is a portion of the more than 1,000 F-4 aircraft that remain in Type 1000 storage. The F-4E/G/RFs will be used as remote-control, ground-operated, air-to-air combat simulators (Drones) that will ultimately be shot down with air-to-air-missiles. The F-4C/Ds will be used as parts donors through a reclamation program, returning parts back into the active inventory. The remainder of the aircraft will be demilitarized, removing all the radioactive parts and turning the aircraft over to DRMO to be sold as scrap to the contractors.

F-4s in impeccable alignment.

F-4E 'Babe' – Missouri Air National Guard, St Louis, MO.

▲ An assorted group of tails of new arrivals representing the combat ready force that is being retired because of the funding constraints. These aircraft represent the RF-4Cs from Bergstrom AFB, TX, the F-111Ds from Clovis AFB, NM and the F-111As from Mountain Home AFB, ID.

▼ This unique F-4 is identified as a YF-4 that was utilized for experimental purposes at Edwards AFB, CA. Note the familiar red painted vertical and horizontal stabilizers and red wing tips that are easily visible for experimental purposes.

▼ Thirty years of jerkin' the Reds, got shot down by the Feds (RF-4C).

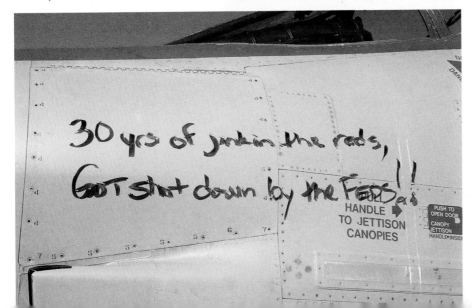

U.S. AIRFORCE F-4E
A.F. SERIAL NO. 71-1086
SERVICE THIS AIRCRAFT WITH
GRADE JP-4 FUEL
IDENTPLATE LOCATION

3TFW

GUNSMOKE 89

TOP F-4 TEAM
F-4 TOP GUN
TOP F-4 MAINTENANCE TEAM
TOP F-4 COMBAT SERVICING TEAM

GUNSMOKE 89

ARMAMENT

▲ F-4E 71-1086 has done very well over the years. Gunsmoke 89 proved its effectiveness with these accolades. The aircraft arrived at AMARC on 3 Mar. 91.

▼ Chopped F-4 fuselages awaiting meltdown at National Aircraft, Tucson, AZ.

Aerial view of F-15s. 2/94

F-15A 73-092 was the first F-15A to arrive at AMARC from the Louisiana Air Guard at New Orleans. These aged F-15As will undergo reclamation to return parts back into the active inventory.

◀ Aerial view of F-16As. 4/95

▲ These F-16A/Bs represent a small portion of the total built for the country of Pakistan. These aircraft arrived at AMARC directly from General Dynamics in Fort Worth, TX, with an average total of seven hours on each aircraft. A total of twenty-seven aircraft will be delivered to AMARC and will remain in storage until the country signs the Nonproliferation Agreement. These are the Block 15 F-16As/Bs made in 1991/1992.

▼ Former Edwards AFB F-16A.

Former Navy Top Gun F-16N.

These OA-37As are recent arrivals from Battle Creek, Michigan. These aircraft are prime candidates for Foreign Military Sales. Some of the first to arrive were disassembled and sent to Peru on C-141s. Two more will go to the Latin American Air Force Academy at Lackland AFB, TX.

Aerial view of AC-130 Gunships. 2/95

▲ Navy TF-9J 147394 awaiting Museum transfer.

▼ A line-up of Douglas F-10D Skynights.

This F-8J is one of eleven that went to France under the Foreign Military Sales Program. France was interested in obtaining the low time wings for use with their F-8Ns which are similar to our F-8Js. Upon closer examination by their engineers from Paris, it was determined not only the wings but the entire aircraft would go. The close examination revealed a corrosion-free aircraft. Eleven aircraft were purchased in 1990 with the remaining nine to follow in 1991; however, the remaining nine did not go and will be used as ground targets in the gunnery ranges.

This A-3 flew from Roto, Spain to be put into storage at AMARC.

▲ Former Marine Aggressor A-4M.

▼ Ominous head-on view of a stored F-14.

F-18A 161716 fresh from duty with the Navy Fighter Weapons
School sits on the Receiving ramp.

AV-8B Harrier begins the preservation process.

▲ A German Tornado enters short term storage. A former participant of the 'Red Flag' operation at Nellis AFB, NV, the German Air Force opted to store the two aircraft at AMARC in lieu of flying them back to Germany.

▲ The T-33As are favored among the foreign countries who convert these previously used trainers to tactical aircraft by installing guns in them. The forty-one shown here are in Type 1000 storage and could be made ready to fly in a short period of time.

▼ A T-34C that was operated by the Army.

▲ Air Force T-37s on the departure ramp.

▼ The prototype T-46 was built by Fairchild to replace the T-37 'Tweety-Bird'. Only three were built. As a result of the Air Force not buying the aircraft, Fairchild declared bankruptcy and was sold to Maryland Air Industries. One was recently sent up to the Air Force Museum at Wright-Patterson AFB, OH.

▲ This is one of many TA-4Js that operated aboard the USS *Lexington*. The TA-4J has been replaced with the T-45 Goshawk.

▼ This black T-38A was previously assigned to the 49th Fighter Wing at Holloman AFB, NM. It was painted black to coordinate with the F-117A Night Hawk 'Stealth Fighter'.

▲ 515165 T-29 Navigator trainer. 8/81

▼ Aerial view of stored T-39s. 2/94

▲ TC-4C in storage, previously used as a bombardier-navigator trainer for A-6s.

PAGES 62 & 63: The following pages depict the B-52s in the START area as the sun sets in the west. The creaking of the rudders and elevators can be heard throughout the area.

▼ Two T-43As arrived at AMARC from Randolph AFB, TX, formerly used as navigator trainers. The aircraft configured as navigator trainers have provisions for twelve navigator trainees, four advanced navigator positions, and three instructors. The T-43A is built on a Boeing 737-200 airframe.

▼ The B-52s methodically positioned in the START area represent a portion of those that will be cut in accordance with the Treaty. Some of them have been here more than twenty-two years, having been through a reclamation program and then made available for priority removals to provide support to the operational units on a priority basis. These B-52s represent a portion of the total strategic force.

▲ This B-52G proudly displays the Diamond K on the tail which indicates the aircraft is from The 379th Bomb Wing at Wurtsmith AFB, Michigan. That tail symbol was a common sight seen flying out of Jeddah, Saudi Arabia during Operation Desert Storm.

▼ B-57C 53-3840 formerly of the Vermont Air National Guard.

▲ This is a one of a kind B-52. This NB-52E was used as a high altitude stability platform. It is unique in that it has J57-43WB engines with alternators on the engines, first used on B-52F aircraft, canards and spoilers and extended pitot boom for more precise pitot readings for the sophisticated electronic equipment on board. It has flaperons (split flaps that act as ailerons), a fuel drain mast from the aft main tank (used in the event of an emergency to dump fuel). The outboard fuel tanks were filled with lead to assist in stabilizing the aircraft at altitude. The bomb bay houses a test platform that flight crew members could occupy in flight. The total flight hours on the aircraft was 1,378. Unfortunately, it will be cut up in accordance with START.

▶ 55-0077, a B-52D displaying the infamous 'Sharkmouth', was operated by the 43rd Bomb Wing at Anderson AFB, Guam. 0077 arrived at AMARC during the last days of July 1983 after accruing 14,679 flight hours. Another unsung hero of the war over North Vietnam.

▲ This Navy C-118 was one of ten that was traded to Mr Carl Enzenhofer of Vancouver, British Colombia.

▼ This Super Constellation was used by the Navy as a flying radar station.

This C-123 was one of four that was flown out for the State Department for the Drug Interdiction program in South America. One was blown up with a fire-bomb in Medellin, Colombia. While the other three continue to operate, AMARC will provide parts from the fourteen donor aircraft assigned to the State Department.

This HC-130B, previously operated by the Coast Guard, was retired on 29 Jul. 82 from Barbers Point, Hawaii. The engines and landing gear were removed and returned to the Coast Guard inventory. These aircraft were very instrumental in providing support to the C-130B fleet.

Convair C-131H N4276C, DOS Air Wing, was used to haul supplies to Lima, Peru, in support of the Drug Interdiction Program for the Department of State.

▲ The VC-140 was a very versatile aircraft, used in a variety of missions. This VIP model was used to ferry high level personnel around the country. More resourceful were the C-140s used to calibrate the Rapcon facilities in Southeast Asia during the Vietnam War. Those C-140s operated out of Clark AB, Philippines.

▼ The C-26 aircraft were operated by the Air National Guard as Operational Support Aircraft. It was configured to carry nineteen passengers or as an air ambulance for medical evacuation missions.

The C-12B was used by the Navy in liaison and communication roles and can carry up to thirteen passengers or up to 2,000 lb of cargo. Hopefully, the C-12B will be returned to service as Foreign Military Sales Candidates or commercial carriers.

Aerial view of stored O-2As. 3/94

In 1965 KC-97J 52-2693 departed AMARC for Long Beach, CA, where it was converted into the Super Guppy, specifically to carry the Saturn IV and V Boosters and the Lunar Module. The Super Guppy has a 25 ft inside diameter, the fuselage having been made from five KC-97s. The hinge points on the forward fuselage allow the whole forward section to be rotated to the left, allowing the cargo to be loaded from the front. The aircraft carries a 41,000 lb payload at 25,000 ft at a speed of 300 knots. It is powered by four T-34 turboprop engines that required the prop blades to be cut off a foot to allow the props to clear the fuselage. Cutting a foot off the prop blades reduced the thrust by 1,500 horsepower.

An impression of the size of the Super Guppy as it is parked in the RIT area among the E-2 Hawkeyes.

Boeing's answer to the STOL competition lifted off in Seattle, Washington on 9 Aug. 76. Although the YC-14 had only two engines, the CF6-50Ds powered out some 102,000 lb of combined thrust. The YC-14 was somewhat larger than the YC-15 by McDonnell Douglas, but both had identical flight characteristics. The cargo areas were also identical at 6,214 sq. ft. With the two engines mounted high and forward of the wings, exhaust was allowed to blast over the upper surfaces of the wings and down the segments of finger shaped flaps under the wings, providing the additional lift, giving the YC-14 true STOL performance.

This former American Airlines 707-300 had previously had its landing gear removed to support the E-3B program. The aircraft had to be moved to another area to consolidate the 707s. An extended trailer device was initiated by the Towing Section to move the 707s with no landing gear. Here the two cranes are preparing to lift the aircraft to allow the extended trailer to be backed up under and rigged for towing.

The HU-16 Albatross and the F-84F are assets of the Air Force Museum.

▲ Vertical stabilizers removed from the 707s are placed in a pile near the 707s. The vertical stabilizers had to be removed prior to removing the engines or the aircraft would set on its tail.

▼ HU-25 Guardian, previously operated by the Coast Guard as Drug Interdiction aircraft. They were configured with side looking radar and intercepted drug runners coming from South America. Funding was limited by the Department of Transportation so the aircraft was retired.

OV-10A Broncos after arrival for storage.

PAGES 78 & 79: Aerial view of a C-141A used for experimental purposes and C-141B cargo aircraft.

E-2B 160415 was operated by the Coast Guard at St Augustine, FA. It was credited with many accomplishments in defeating the Drug Cartel. It advocates saying 'NO' to drugs. 508 is responsible for apprehending fifty-two people, eight boats and nineteen aircraft. The aircraft is being retired due to lack of funds to operate.

▲ S-3A 160594 Viking off the carrier USS *Kittyhawk*.

▼ US-2B from Alameda Naval Air Station rests in storage.

▲ These P-2V Neptunes have been sold through DRMO.

▼ P-3 149670 operated by the Naval Research Laboratory.

This P-3 is one of five that were cargo configured and operated in the Arctic in support of the Navy Expedition. Pictured here is the World Traveler 'The Loon'. Also stored at AMARC is 'Arctic Fox' and 'The Tasmanian Devil'.

WB-57F high altitude weather aircraft that operated above 70,000 ft with TF-33-11 engines as main engines with the J-60 engines under the wings. The aircraft was modified from its original design from the B-57E Canberra.

Navy HH-1H 158230.

The Coast Guard converting to HH-60 helicopters has left these HH-3Es excess to the inventory. The helos are in Type 4000 storage and will be disposed of in the near future. Other HH-3Es were routed to Elizabeth City, NC, the Coast Guard Depot where all essential parts required in the Coast Guard inventory were removed and the hulks were routed to AMARC for disposal.

AH-1J Gunship 157801 arrived at AMARC on 5 Aug. 92.

The H-54 'Skycrane' is capable of lifting 22,400 lb and was used extensively during the Vietnam War. It flew to AMARC from Reno, NV and will be used as trading material by the Air Force Museum.

IIG Tanks, Missiles, Special Tooling, and Other Miscellaneous Storage Items

▼ The M-60 tanks in the foreground are being replaced by the M1A1 Abrams tank in the background. The new M1A1s were temporary residents of AMARC until they were trucked to Fort Huachuca to replace the ageing M-60s that will go back to the depot for rework, and then be made available for Foreign Military Sales.

This ground launched cruise missile (GLCM) contained a piece of titanium that had to be cut with a torch. The rest of the missile was cut with a K-12 saw with a carbon steel rotating blade prior to being turned over to DRMO for sale as scrap metal.

This is a GLCM launcher that holds four missiles. These launchers were flown to AMARC from Europe aboard C-5Bs to be cut up in accordance with the INF treaty. AMARC cut up 125 launchers in accordance with the treaty.

This enclosed facility represents the Elimination site for the ground launched cruise missiles (GLCM) that were deactivated in Europe under the Intermediate-Range Nuclear Forces (INF) Treaty. A total of 445 missiles and 125 launchers were cut up under the surveillance of the Soviets. Over 30,645 man-hours were expended during the elimination without a reportable mishap. Twenty-seven line items were removed from each missile and returned to the active Navy inventory to support their Trident and Polaris missiles.

Manufactured by Lockheed, the D-21 Drone was designed to be launched from atop the SR-71 Blackbird at a speed of Mach 2. These seventeen D-21 Drones in storage were never used and now have been turned over to the Air Force Museum for static displays.

▲ ZPG-3W 144243 was an aircraft warning device that operated off the coast of New Jersey from 1965 through 1969. The gondola is lined with radar operators stations on both sides. It has a crew comfort pallet that sits on top in the front which contains a galley and bunks for the crew. There is a radar antenna that sits on the back. The balloon contains 1,500,000 cu. ft of helium and was struck by lightning while it was moored to the ground at Lakehurst Naval Air Station, NJ, in 1969. The unit now belongs to the Smithsonian Air and Space Museum and will eventually be displayed at the Dulles Airport Museum Annex.

This is all that remains of fifteen F-100 parts donors for the QF-100 Drone Program. These aircraft were essential in providing parts to put 312 F-100s back into the air as QF-100s.

▲ One of AMARC's greatest attributes is the capability to properly and safely package aircraft parts for distribution throughout the world. This conveyor is routed from the maintenance side of the house where each part is thoroughly inspected and condition coded after being routed through the NDI process and appropriately tagged according to the condition of the part requested. The part is then routed through the Supply inspection section where it is again inspected and the condition code is verified. Then the part is routed to the packaging section where they have the capability to make cardboard containers of all sizes to fit the part and will foam pack, if required, according to MILSPECS. From this area the part is routed to the shipping section where it is processed and shipped to the depot for rework or to an operational unit for immediate use.

▼ This C-130B forward crew compartment is on its way to the Lockheed facility at Marietta, Georgia, where it will be used to form, fit, and function the cockpit for a newly developed C-130J. The crew compartment was cut at sta. 245 plus four inches to accommodate a full-up operational cockpit.

▲ Military technicians practise sheet metal repair on this A-10A
airframe in AIRCRAFT BATTLE DAMAGE REPAIR school.

▼ This C-130B nose section and left hand main landing gear section
have been removed for modification as future training aids.

▲ This C-130B is being prepared to move down the highway intact to Fort Chaffee, Arkansas, to be used by the Joint Readiness Training Center as a Loadmaster trainer by the Army and Air Force. Snyder Trucking Company provides the strongback fixture that attaches to the inside of the fuselage. A set of wheels attaches to the floor forward of the cargo ramp and supports the rear of the fuselage. Eighty-nine feet of fuselage will go down the highway intact.

▼ The forward section of this F-4C was removed and sent to Sheppard AFB, TX, for use as a simulator. Many times AMARC is called upon to provide props and locations for movies or cockpits for use as simulators for combat units to train maintenance personnel.

▲ EC-135G 62-3570, previously a launch control center is now
completely deskinned to accommodate a corrosion analysis project at
Oklahoma City ALC, under the supervision of Lt Col Don Nieser.

▼ 'Hi MOM', another B-52 used by the Wright Laboratories for
explosive testing to determine a type material that would contain an
airborne explosion.

▲ This MIG-15 was part of a Tri-Service project that was later terminated. The aircraft was stored at AMARC until considered excess. It was later transferred to the Air Force Museum account and later assigned for static display at the Pima Air and Space Museum.

◄ Former American Airlines 707 used by the Wright Laboratories for explosive testing to determine a type material that would contain an airborne explosion.

▼ This disassembled F-100F was returned from the Mojave Desert after it was declared excess when the drone contract had terminated. There were eleven aircraft that were returned to AMARC, six flying home and the other five being disassembled and trucked home due to the amount of parts that were removed. The aircraft have been made available as static display aircraft for the Air Force Museum.

The HU-16s assigned to AMARC are museum assets used for trading purposes. This HU-16D belongs to the Air Force Museum and is available for trade.

Lockheed P-2H 147963 has been in storage at AMARC since 1975. It is the property of the Smithsonian Air and Space Museum. After sixteen years in storage the aircraft was represerved, removing the spraylat and filling the aircraft with fuel. The engines were run and all systems were operated and the aircraft was confirmed as being fully operational for flight. The storage process was again implemented and the aircraft was returned to storage until AMARC is notified to prepare the aircraft for flight by the Smithsonian.

△ This B-57F arrived at AMARC in Oct. 82 after faithful service with NASA. The engines were removed and the highly sophisticated electronic equipment was removed from the cockpit and the aircraft was made available to the Pima Air and Space Museum.

▽ AV-8A Harrier nose crated for shipment.

The B-52 has carried on the nose art tradition from its ancestral bombers of WWII. This Aug. 90 arrival from Castle AFB, CA, is typical of the B-52s bearing nose art.

'Against the Wind', B-52G 57-6499 arrived at AMARC on 7 Aug. 90 from the 93rd Bomb Wing, Castle AFB, CA. The Crew Chief was SSgt L. Coleman, the Asst Crew Chief was SRA R. Barrett, A1C T Bissette, and AMN. B. Hardin. The artwork was airbrushed by SSgt Ron Cooke, 93rd OMS, Castle AFB, CA. 6499 had a total of 15,316 flight hours.

'Alley Oops Bold Assault', B-52G 58-0159 proved its worth by flying forty-six sorties over Iraq during Operation Desert Storm. 0159 arrived at AMARC on 9 Oct. 92. 0159 had a total of 14,123 flight hours.

▷ 'Better Duck II', B-52G 59-2590 arrived at AMARC on 13 Jul. 92 from the 379th Bomb Wing at Wurtsmith AFB, MI with a total of 14,495 flight hours.

◁ 'Buffasaurus', B-B52G 58-0194 arrived at AMARC on 10 Oct. 91 from the 2nd Bomb Wing, Barksdale AFB, LA, with a total of 12,942 flight hours.

▷ 'City of Merced', B-52G 58-0207, arrived at AMARC on 25 Jul. 91 from the 93rd Bomb Wing, Castle AFB, CA. This meticulous piece of artwork was airbrushed by SSgt Ron Cooke, 93rd OMS at Castle. This unique nose art shows Batman in the lower left hand window as you climb up the stairs. 0207 had a total of 14,027 flight hours.

◁ 'Damage Inc.', B-52G 58-0254 arrived at AMARC on 4 Dec. 90 from the 93rd Bomb Wing, Castle AFB, CA. Truly a work of art airbrushed by SSgt Ron Cooke, 93rd OMS, Castle AFB, CA. 0254 had a total of 14,363 flight hours.

'Disaster Master', B-52G 58-0232 arrived at AMARC on 3 Apr. 90 from the 42nd Bomb Wing, Loring AFB, ME. The complete nose section was cut off and sent to Randolph AFB, TX, where it will be used as an ejection seat trainer. 0232 had a total of 17,949 flight hours.

'Eternal Guardian', B-52G 58-0195 arrived at AMARC on 18 Nov. 93 with a total of 13,947 flight hours.

'Guardian of Peace', B-52G 58-0255 arrived at AMARC on 28 Oct. 93 with a total of 13,349 flight hours. 0255 flew fifty-five combat sorties over Iraq in Operation Desert Storm.

'Hellsadroppin', B-52G 58-0244 arrived at AMARC on 29 Oct. 92 with a total of 14,400 flight hours.

'High Roller', B-52G 58-0231 arrived at AMARC on 2 Dec. 92 with a total of 13,835 flight hours.

'Hoosier Hot Shot', B-52G 57-6486 arrived at AMARC from the 2nd Bomb Wing, Barksdale AFB, LA, with a total of 18,199 flight hours.

'Large Marge', B-52G 59-2575 arrived at AMARC on 6 Aug. 91 from the 93rd Bomb Wing, Castle AFB, CA with a total of 16,781 flight hours.

'Leo II', B-52G 57-6518 arrived at AMARC on 23 Apr. 91 from the 2nd Bomb Wing, Barksdale AFB, LA, with a total of 13,246 flight hours.

'Let's Make a Deal', B-52G 58-0173 arrived at AMARC on 5 Aug. 92 from the 2nd Bomb Wing, Barksdale AFB, LA with a total of 14,331 flight hours.

'Lil Peach II', B-52G 58-0171 arrived at AMARC on 16 Aug. 90 from the 2nd Bomb Wing, Barksdale AFB, LA with a total of 13,872 flight hours.

'The Lonestar Lady', B-52D 55-0067 from the 7th Bomb Wing, Carswell AFB, TX was selected to represent the B-52D fleet at the Pima Air and Space Museum, Tucson, AZ.

'Lone Wolf', B-52G 57-6474 arrived at AMARC on 15 Oct. 91 From Wurtsmith AFB, MI, a former member of the 379th Bomb Wing. The red/yellow numbers on the EVS pod indicate it is the 265th B-52 assigned as a START aircraft. The 'A' indicates it was an air launched cruise missile carrier and the 'G' indicates it as being a B-52G. These numbers/letters are assigned to each aircraft for the Soviets to be able to identify the type B-52 that is being destroyed in accordance with START. 6474 had a total of 11,386 flight hours.

'Lucky 13', B-52G 58-0236 arrived at AMARC on 13 Oct. 92 from Barksdale AFB, LA with a total of 16,362 flight hours.

'Memphis Belle III', B-52G 59-2594 arrived at AMARC on 15 Oct. 92 from Barksdale AFB, LA. The nose art is reminiscent of World War II and, in spite of the fact that this aircraft will be cut up in accordance with START, the traditional 'Memphis Belle IV' will be displayed on the nose of a B-52H presently assigned to Barksdale AFB, LA.

'Miami Clipper II', B-52G 57-6475 arrived at AMARC on 20 Aug. 91 from the 2nd Bomb Wing, Barksdale AFB, LA. 6475 was the No. 4 of the seven ship formation engaged in the secret mission code named 'Secret Squirrel' from Barksdale AFB, LA to Baghdad, Iraq and return to Barksdale AFB for a record 34 hour sortie. The aircraft flew a non-standard formation of one mile apart with a 500 ft altitude separation. These specially equipped aircraft flew directly to Baghdad, Iraq and launched their air launched cruise missiles with conventional warheads, commencing the start of Operation Desert Storm. The Flight crew consisted of: Aircraft Commander Capt. Bernard S. Morgan; Pilot 1Lt Michael C. Branche; Pilot Augmentee Capt. Steven E Bass; Radar Navigator Capt. John S Ladner; Navigator 1Lt Andre J. Mouton; Navigator Augmentee Maj. Wesley R. Bain; Electronic Warfare Officer Capt. James L. Morris III; Gunner A1C Guy W. Modgling. Crew E-83. 6475 had a total of 12,649 flight hours.

'Miss Fit II', B-52G 58-0238 arrived at AMARC on 20 Aug. 91 from the 2nd Bomb Wing, Barksdale AFB, LA. 0238 was the No. 5 ship in the 'Secret Squirrel' formation. The Flight crew consisted of: Aircraft Commander Capt. Marcus S. Myers; Pilot 1Lt Michael C. Hansen; Pilot Augmentee Capt. Chadwick H. Barr Jr; Radar Navigator Capt. David J. Byrd; Navigator 1Lt Don E. Broyles; Navigator Augmentee Capt. Donald Van Slambrook; Electronic Warfare Officer Capt. Todd H. Mathes; Gunner Sgt Martin R. Van Buren. Crew E-81. 0238 had a total of 13,469 flight hours.

'Miss Ouachita II', B-52G 58-0184 arrived at AMARC on 26 Sept. 91 from the 2nd Bomb Wing, Barksdale AFB, LA with a total of 16,108 flight hours.

'Miss Wing Ding II', B-52G 57-6485 arrived at AMARC on 20 Dec. 90 from the 2nd Bomb Wing, Barksdale AFB, LA with a total of 14,468 flight hours.

'Mohawk Warrior', B-52G 57-6515 arrived at AMARC on 30 Sept. 92 from the 2nd Bomb Wing, Barksdale AFB, LA, with a total of 14,121 flight hours.

'Night Hawk VI', B-52G 58-0220 arrived at AMARC on 5 Jul. 90 from Castle AFB, CA. Another beautiful piece of airbrush work by SSgt Ron Cooke, 93rd OMS, Castle AFB, CA. 0220 had a total of 14,527 flight hours.

▶ 'Old Crow Express', B-52G 57-6492 represented the 379th Bomb Wing well during Operation Desert Storm. 6492 was flown to AMARC as the last B-52G to depart Wurtsmith AFB, MI on 15 Dec. 92. The aircraft was flown by the Wing Commander, Col Bill Campbell with Capt. Barry Sebring as pilot and Capt. Mark Schlechte as co-pilot. 6492 flew fifty-four missions over Iraq. After soaking the Wing Commander down with a water fire extinguisher to celebrate his last flight in a B-52G, a bottle of champagne was opened by Col Campbell and passed around to all present. The champagne was provided by the author, Jerry Fugere. 6492 had a total of 15,084 flight hours.

◀ 'Petie 3rd', B-52G 58-0177 arrived at AMARC on 9 May 91 from the 2nd Bomb Wing, Barksdale AFB, LA. 0177 was the lead aircraft of the 'Secret Squirrel' formation. The Flight crew consisted of: Aircraft Commander Capt. Michael G. Wilson; Pilot 1Lt Kent R. Beck; Pilot Augmentee and Airborne Commander Lt Col Joseph H. Beard; Radar Navigator Capt. George W. Murray, III; Navigator Capt. Mark W. Van Doran; Navigator Augmentee Capt. Lee S. Richie; Electronic Warfare Officer Capt. Richard P. Holt; Gunner Sgt Dale R. Jackson. Crew S-91. 0177 had a total of 14,229 flight hours.

▶ 'Ragin' Cajun', B-52G 57-6483 arrived at AMARC on 19 Sept. 91 from the 2nd Bomb Wing, Barksdale AFB, LA. Another fantastic piece of airbrush work by SSgt Ron Cooke, 93rd OMS, Castle AFB, CA. 6483 had a total of 15,472 flight hours.

◀ 'Ragin' Red', B-52G 57-6501 arrived at AMARC on 3 Oct. 91 from the 416th Bomb Wing, Griffiss AFB, NY. Note the mission symbols (bombs) that depict the number of sorties flown over Iraq during Operation Desert Storm. 6501 had a total of 17,780 flight hours.

'Royal Flush', B-52G 57-6514 arrived at AMARC on 10 Oct. 90 from the 93rd Bomb Wing, Castle AFB, CA, with a total of 16,401 flight hours.

'Sagittarius II', B-52G 58-0252 arrived at AMARC on 18 Apr. 91 from the 2nd Bomb Wing, Barksdale AFB, LA, with a total of 13,109 flight hours.

'Screaming for Vengeance', B-52G 57-6470 arrived at AMARC on 23 Oct. 90 from the 93rd Bomb Wing, Castle AFB, CA. Only an artist like SSgt Ron Cooke, 93rd OMS, Castle AFB, CA, could produce a masterpiece of this sort. 6470 had a total of 13,438 flight hours.

'Sioux Warrior', B-52G 58-0229 arrived at AMARC on 12 Nov. 92 from 2nd Bomb Wing, Barksdale AFB, LA, with a total of 13,598 flight hours.

▶ 'Special Delivery II', B-52G 58-0170 arrived at AMARC on 10 Nov. 92 from the 2nd Bomb Wing, Barksdale AFB, LA. 0170 flew 20 sorties over Iraq during Operation Desert Storm. 0170 had a total of 13,521 flight hours.

◀ 'Specter', B-52G 58-0199 arrived at AMARC on 4 Jun. 91 from the 93rd Bomb Wing, Castle AFB, CA. The aircraft Crew Chief was SSgt J. McKean, Asst Crew Chiefs SRA J. Irwin and SRA R. Hudson. 'Specter' was airbrushed by SSgt Ron Cooke, 93rd OMS, Castle AFB, CA. 0199 had a total of 14,751 flight hours.

▶ 'Spirit of America', B-52G 58-0223 arrived at AMARC on 31 Jul. 90 from the 93rd Bomb Wing, Castle AFB, CA. The nose art was airbrushed by SSgt Ron Cooke, 93rd OMS, Castle AFB, CA. All the nose art on the B-52Gs will be cut out and sent to the Air Force Museum at Wright-Patterson AFB, OH for static display. 0223 had a total of 15,268 flight hours.

◀ 'Stars and Stripes', B-52G 57-6478 arrived at AMARC on 27 Jun. 89 from the 320th Bomb Wing, Mather AFB, CA, with a total of 13,313 flight hours.

'Superstitious Aloysius', B-52G 57-6503 arrived at AMARC on 19 Aug. 92 from Barksdale AFB, LA, with a total of 15,581 flight hours.

'Swashbuckler', B-52G 59-2585 arrived at AMARC on 15 Apr. 93 from the 42nd Bomb Wing, Loring AFB, ME. 2585 flew twenty-two combat sorties in Operation Desert Storm. Capt. Gregg Davis flew the aircraft to its resting place, where it will be cut up in accordance with START. 2585 had a total of 13,989 flight hours.

'Sweet Revenge', B-52G 59-2591 arrived at AMARC on 19 Jun. 92 from the 2nd Bomb Wing, Barksdale AFB, LA, with a total of 14,626 flight hours.

'Tantalizing Takeoff', B-52G 57-6471 arrived at AMARC on 29 Jul. 92 from the 2nd Bomb Wing, Barksdale AFB, LA, with a total of 13,214 flight hours.

'Ultimate Warrior', B-52G 57-6516 arrived at AMARC on 8 Oct. 91 as the last B-52G to depart Griffiss AFB, NY. The aircraft was flown by the Wing Commander, Col Mike Laughrin. A veteran of Operation Desert Storm, 6516 flew twelve sorties over Iraq. Many stories can be told about this aircraft by the author, Jerry Fugere, who was the actual Crew Chief in 1965-66 at Dow AFB, ME. In March 1968, the 397th Bomb Wing at Dow AFB, ME was deactivated and joined the 2nd Bomb Wing at Barksdale AFB, LA. 6516 had a total of 15,566 flight hours.

'Triple Deuce', B-52G 58-0222 arrived at AMARC on 12 Aug. 92 from the 2nd Bomb Wing, Barksdale AFB, LA, with a total of 16,560 flight hours.

'Valkyrie', B-52G 58-0183 arrived at AMARC on 9 Jul. 91 from the 2nd Bomb Wing, Barksdale AFB, LA. 0183 was the No. 6 ship in the 'Secret Squirrel' formation. The aircraft is presently located at the Pima Air and Space Museum, Tucson, AZ. The Flight crew consisted of: Aircraft Commander Capt. Alan W. Moe; Pilot Capt. David T Greer, Jr; Pilot Augmentee Capt. Joseph M. Hasbrouck; Radar Navigator Capt. Blaise M Martinick; Navigator 1Lt John S Pyles; Navigator Augmentee Capt. Matthew G Cassella; Electronic Warfare Officer Capt. Anthony Bothwell; Gunner Sgt Danny L. Parker; additional Pilot Maj. Steven D Weilbrenner. Crew S-92. 0183 had a total of 13,297 flight hours.

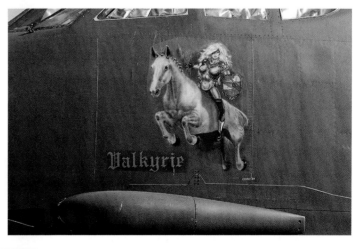

'Viper', B-52G 58-0175 arrived at AMARC on 16 Oct. 91 with a total of 14,413 flight hours.

'What's Up, Doc?', B-52G 58-0182 arrived at AMARC on 10 Jun. 92 from the 379th Bomb Wing, Wurtsmith AFB, MI, with a total of 8,768 flight hours.

'The Wild Hare 2', B-52G 58-0205 arrived at AMARC on 15 Nov. 90 from the 2nd Bomb Wing, Barksdale AFB, LA, with a total of 13,459 flight hours.

'Wild Thing', B-52G 57-6486 arrived at AMARC on 15 Aug. 91 from 93rd Bomb Wing, Castle AFB, CA, with a total of 15,737 flight hours.

'Yankee Doodle II', B-52G 59-2602 arrived at AMARC on 27 Oct. 92 with a total of 16,070 flight hours.

No, it's not a palm tree, it's a bomb tree! Having replaced the coconuts with bombs, the 43rd Bomb Wing at Anderson AFB, Guam, always felt confident the mission would be a success.

B-52G 58-0178 displays nose art that is truly a work of art. The 'Old Soldier' was airbrushed by SSgt Ron Cooke, 93rd Bomb Wing, Castle AFB, CA. Although the painting was duplicated on a piece of aircraft metal by Mr Randy Walker of Oklahoma City, OK, for General Charles McDonald, Commander of the Air Force Logistics Command, on his retirement, it reminisced the adage 'Old Soldiers Never Die, They Just Fade Away'. The original painting is, in fact, fading away more every day. The aircraft was assigned to Mather AFB, CA, when Gen. McDonald was Wing Commander. The painting is being held by the author, Jerry Fugere. 0178 had a total of 14,241 flight hours.

'Big Bad Boom', KC-135A 56-03637 arrived at AMARC on 6 Aug. 92 from the 410th Bomb Wing, K.I. Sawyer AFB, MI, with a total of 15,099 flight hours.

B-52G nose art cut from the aircraft to be preserved by the Air Force Museum.

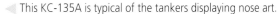
This KC-135A is typical of the tankers displaying nose art.

'Boss Hog', KC-135A 56-3625 arrived at AMARC on 5 May 93 from the 96th Bomb Wing, Dyess AFB, TX, with a total of 11,752 flight hours.

'Swamp Rat III', KC-135A 56-03636 arrived at AMARC on 28 Jul. 92 from the 2nd Bomb Wing, Barksdale AFB, LA, with a total of 12,061 flight hours.

'Jolly Roger', KC-135A 58-0097 arrived at AMARC on 8 Sept. 92 with a total of 14,279 flight hours.

▲ 'The Last of the Best' KC-135A 58-0110 arrived at AMARC with a total of 12,497 flight hours.

▲ 'Bustin' Out', KC-135A 56-03646 arrived at AMARC with a total of 10,806 flight hours.

◄ KC-135A 62-3501 'Young Tiger', a mission calling the tankers into action to refuel the fighters operating out of Thailand to strike well into Vietnam. 1967–68 found the author serving his flight crews prime IF10 dinners while *en route* to the IP.

▶ 'Freedom's Best', KC-135A 56-3634 arrived at AMARC on 22 Sept. 92 with a total of 15,438 flight hours.

◀ 'Running Free', KC-135A 62-3539 arrived at AMARC with a total of 12,607 flight hours.

▶ 'Thunder Chicken', NKC-135A 55-03127 displays the insignia of the 4950th Test Wing, Wright-Patterson AFB, OH. 3127 arrived at AMARC with a total of 11,356 flight hours.

◀ 'Thunder Chicken', an NKC-135A from the 4950th Test Wing, Wright-Patterson AFB, OH. 55-03127 was one of the oldest -135As operating.

▶ The nose art on EC-135H 61-0291 represents the lion defending the British Isles. The aircraft was formerly assigned to Mildenhall AFB, England.

▲ 'Stone Age Mutant Ninja Tanker', KC-135A 56-3633 arrived at AMARC with a total of 11,743 flight hours.

▲ 'Aurora Explorer', an NC-135A displays the logo of the 4950th Test Wing, Wright-Patterson AFB, OH.

▽ NKC-135A 56-03596 one of two NKC-135As assigned to the Navy to undertake electronic warfare simulation duties. Both aircraft are equipped with ECM jammers under the wings.

▽ Widespread application of nose art on the A-10 was a product of Desert Storm.

'Steam Jet One'. EC-135C 63-8047 arrived at AMARC with a total of 21,667 flight hours.

'Yankee Express', is proudly displayed on an OA-10 from Alconbury, England. These tank-killers were very instrumental in determining the outcome of Operation Desert Storm, the 100 day war in Iraq.

'Aimee Larry II'.

'Randi Lauren' 'Brenda Beth', A-10A 77-0240 arrived at AMARC on 17 Aug. 92 with a total of 8,184 flight hours.

926th Ftr Gp logo for Desert Storm.

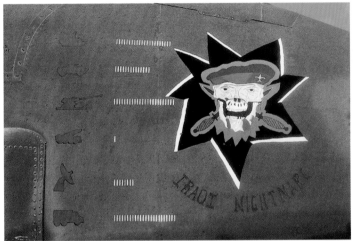

'Iraqi Nightmare', New Orleans A-10A.

'Crescent City's Desert Darly', A-10A 77-0268 arrived at AMARC on 26 Oct. 92 with a total of 3,700 flight hours.

'Desert Storm Heroes', New Orleans A-10A.

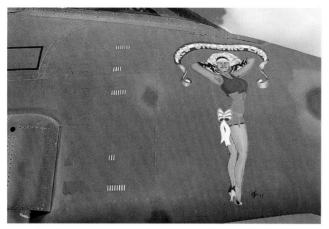

'New Orleans Lady', New Orleans A-10A.

▼ 'Desert Rose' is a proud example of the nose art displayed on A-10A 77- 0273 from the New Orleans 926th Ftr Gp. It exemplifies the participation of the 926th in Operation Desert Storm. On the left are the credited kills of this one particular aircraft.

▼ Although many organizations prohibited the painting of nose art many crew chiefs took the initiative to paint the inside door of the entrance ladder on the A-10A. Here is an excellent piece of art work entitled 'Primal Scream'.

▼ 'Sweet Meat', A-10A 79-0220 arrived at AMARC on 28 Jan. 92 from Alconbury, England with a total of 4,123 flight hours.

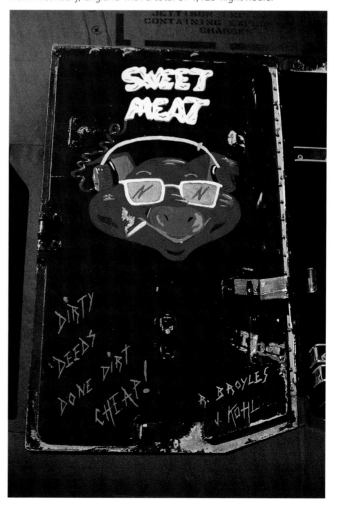

▲ 'Battlin' Badger', A-10A.

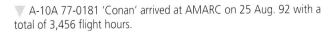

▲ 'Spirit of Chicago'.

▼ A-10A 77-0181 'Conan' arrived at AMARC on 25 Aug. 92 with a total of 3,456 flight hours.

▼ 'Death from Above', A-10A.

'Dragon Lady', F-4.

'Arizona or Bust', arrived at AMARC on 24 Oct. 90.

'Acme Flight Test' F-15A 77-084 (Edwards AFB, CA).

RF-4C 64-01066 'Miss Photo Genic' arrived at AMARC on 25 Feb. 92 from the 155th TRG, Lincoln MAP (ANG) Lincoln, NE, with a total of 6,165 flight hours. 1066 was assigned as the Commander, Col Bruce Schantzs' aircraft. Col Schantz had flown 1066 earlier in his career at Ramstein AB, Germany. The crew chiefs assigned to 1066 include TSgt Tim Craig and SSgt Doug Otto.

▲ F-4G 69-7211 arrived at AMARC on 14 Feb. 96 with a total of 5,594 flight hours.

▲ 'Sturgis Bound Hawg Wild', RF-4C 65-0824 arrived at AMARC on 12 Jul. 93 with a total of 6,855 flight hours.

▶ 'Defender of Freedom', RF-4C 65-0931 arrived at AMARC on 22 Sep. 93 with a total of 5,952 flight hours.

◀ RF-4C 64-01062 'Free Spirit' arrived at AMARC on 25 Feb. 92 from the 155th TRG, Lincoln MAP (ANG), Lincoln, NE, with a total of 5,473 flight hours. SSgt Jeff Marshall, who was the crew chief and also the artist of 'Free Spirit', was later killed in an auto accident.

RF-4C 'Mystic Mission Miss Emily'.

'Elmer', RF-4C 65-0828 arrived at AMARC on 12 Jul. 93 with a total of 6887 flight hours.

'Girls Just Wanna Have Fun', RF-4C 66-0418 arrived at AMARC on 28 Jul. 93 with a total of 6,522 flight hours.

'D. I. Joe', RF-4C 65-0838 arrived at AMARC on 30 Aug. 93 with a total of 6121 flight hours.

▲ 'Betty Boop', RF-4C 65-0859 arrived at AMARC on 19 May 94 with a total of 5,937 flight hours.

▲ 'Outlaw', RF-4C 65-0928 arrived at AMARC on 26 Jul. 93 with a total of 6,500 flight hours.

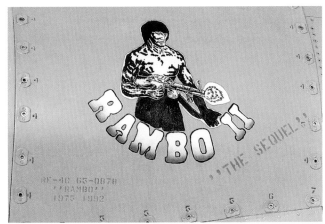

▲ 'Rambo II', RF-4C 66-0428 arrived at AMARC on 16 Sep. 93 with a total of 7,591 flight hours.

▼ 'Rambo', RF-4C 65-0878 arrived at AMARC on 14 Jan. 92 with a total of 6,730 flight hours.

‘Better Than The Best’, RF-4C 64-0055 arrived at AMARC on 14 Apr. 94 with a total of 7,462 flight hours.

‘ANG Phirst in Phantoms’, RF-4C 65-0867 arrived at AMARC on 28 Apr. 94 with a total of 6,570 flight hours.

‘Kodak Moment’, RF-4C 66-0400 arrived at AMARC on 26 May 94 with a total of 6,656 flight hours.

‘057 First In, Last Out’, RF-4C 64-1057 arrived at AMARC on 26 May 94 with a total of 6,823 flight hours.

▲ RF-4C 65-0843 of the 117th Recon Wing, 106th TRS, Birmingham, AL Air National Guard in its entirety. This beautiful work of art will be situated on Celebrity Row at AMARC to expound on its accomplishments for the past seventy-five years. The aircraft could ultimately be assigned as an air-to-air combat simulator (Drone) in the coming years.

▲ 'Phantoms Phorever', RF-4C 64-1058 arrived at AMARC on 14 Apr. 94 with a total of 5,946 flight hours.

▶ RFC-4C 65-0843.

◀ 65-0843.

RF-4C 64-1057 arrived at AMARC on 26 May 94 with a total of 6,823 flight hours.

This unique nose art is displayed on F-106B 59-0043 depicting the personal relationship that the 177th FIS of Atlantic City, NJ, had with this record setter, which established a high speed record of 1,525.5 miles per hour on 15 Dec. 1959.

'Farewell', F-111F from 524th Ftr Squadron.

'Miss Liberty', F-111F 74-0187 had tears in her eyes as the last F-111 is retired from active military service. 0187 arrived at AMARC on 29 Jul. 96 with a total of 2,773 flight hours.

'77th Gambler's Last Deal', F-111E 68-049 arrived at AMARC from Upper Heyford, England on 13 Oct. 93 with a total of 5,454 flight hours.

'Last Roll of the Dice', F-111E 68-061 arrived at AMARC from Upper Heyford, England on 8 Dec. 93 with a total of 5,707 flight hours.

'Peace Offering', FB-111A.

'Moonlight Maid', FB-111A 67-0163 arrived at AMARC on 2 Jul. 91 from the 528th Bomb Sq., 380 Bomb Wing, Plattsburg AFB, NY. 0163 had a total of 6,476 flight hours. The assigned pilot was Capt. Nelson and the crew chief was SSgt Lauzon. The nose art on the FB-111As was reminiscent of the 528th and 529th Bomb Squadrons that originated at Davis-Monthan AFB, AZ in 1942 with B-24s.

'Shy-Chi Baby', FB-111A 68-0251 arrived at AMARC on 1 Jul. 91 from the 528th Bomb Sq., 380th Bomb Wing, Plattsburg AFB, NY. 0251 had a total of 5,534 flight hours. The assigned pilot was Capt. Young and the crew chief was Sgt Blackwell.

'Slightly Dangerous', FB-111A 67-7192 arrived at AMARC on 2 Jul. 91 from the 528th Bomb Sq., 380th Bomb Wing, Plattsburg AFB, NY. 7192 had a total of 6,355 flight hours. The assigned pilot was Capt. Watson and the crew chief was Sgt Henshaw.

'Little Joe' FB-111A 68-0249 arrived at AMARC on 10 Jul. 91, flown by the Wing Commander of the 380th Bomb Wing, Plattsburg AFB, NY, Col Joe Malandrino. 'Little Joe', the last FB-111A to arrive at AMARC, had a total of 6,105 flight hours.

A-7D 71-0371 from the 192nd Tactical Ftr Wg.

'Thumper', A-7D 72-0223 arrived at AMARC from the Virginia Air National Guard, Richmond, VA.

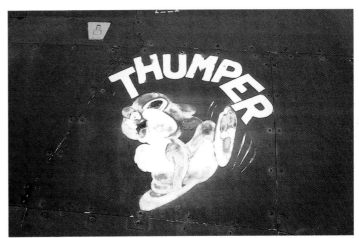

'Happy Hour Four', A-7D 71-0376 arrived from the Virginia Air National Guard, Richmond, VA.

When the 185th Ftr Gp converted to F-16s, they brought their A-7Ds to AMARC to be put into storage. It was unique that each A-7D had a different high school logo painted on the side. The South Sioux City Cardinals is painted on the side of this A-7D.

This memory of 'Memphis Belle' was depicted on the side of a C-130A that arrived at AMARC from the 164th Tactical Airlift Gp, an Air Force Reserve unit from Memphis, TN. C-130A 57-0463 arrived at AMARC on 7 Jan. 92.

'City of Tucson' was proudly displayed on a C-130A from the 162nd Air National Guard, Tucson International Airport, Tucson, AZ.

'Night Stalker', AC-130A.

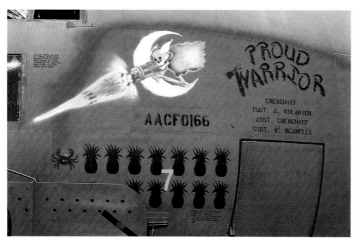

'Proud Warrior', AC-130A.

EC-130Q 156173.

EC-130Q 156173.

'True Tacamo Warrior', EC-130Q 156173 arrived at AMARC on 6 Jun. 90 in exchange for an E-6B.

EC-130Q 156172.

'The Gambler', NC-141A 61-2777 was previously assigned to the 4950th Test Wing, Wright-Patterson AFB, OH. 2777 arrived at AMARC on 27 Sep. 94 with a total of 5,254 flight hours.

'The Loon' is easily recognized on the nose of this UP-3A converted to a cargo aircraft and operated in the Arctic as a World Traveler. Also included as World Travelers were 'The Tasmanian Devil' and 'Arctic Fox' which was later transferred under the Foreign Military Sales to Chile.

'Killer Whales' is displayed on the side of this EA-3 from Rota, Spain.

Among the many nose arts provided by the Navy is the A-6B 501, displaying this outstanding picture of 'Puff the Magic Dragon'.

SH-2F 150179 arrived at AMARC on 9 Dec. 92. It operated from the deck of the USS/G. *Philip* in Central America.

'Orient Express' illustrates the crew responsible for operating, as well as maintaining, the SH-2F that operated aboard the *USS John A Moore* in the Pacific.

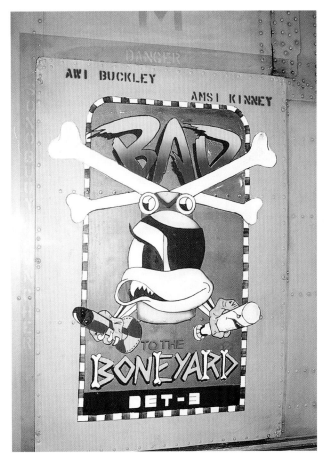

'To the Boneyard'.

▽ HSL-33.

▽ 'Just Call Me Fifi'.

IV
SCRAPPING THE B-52

At the foot of the Rincon Mountains the B-52s remain lined up awaiting their turn for the guillotine. The prototype, cut up for START, has already had the forward fuselage hauled away and the wings and 47 section remain. Everything will be cut into smaller sections to expedite the move.

PAGES 142 & 143: On 5 Apr. 93, Capt. Ron Neville, 92nd Bomb Wing, Fairchild AFB, WA, flew his last flight in a B-52H after participating in the Arizona and Aviation Days at Davis-Monthan AFB, Tucson, AZ. Here he pays tribute by dipping his wings to those who preceded him and his mighty B-52H by assembling at AMARC to be sacrificed by being cut up in accordance with START. Those that preceded him saw much action in Vietnam flying the Rolling Thunder missions in 1965, the Linebacker sorties over North Vietnam in 1969 and 1972 and the Desert Storm sorties over Iraq in 1991. Many decades have passed since the making of the 1954 B-52Cs and the 1961 B-52Hs that made the flyby.

▲ The final prototype cut was accomplished on 5 Feb. 92. The cut was viewed from a helicopter from the 71st Special Operations Sq. The aft section in the foreground is one that was left over from the elimination during SALT II.

PAGES 144 & 145: Aerial view of the B-52s. 10/93

▼ This is the final configuration of the B-52E cut up in accordance with START. The aircraft will remain in this configuration for a period of 90 days, allowing the Soviet satellites to take pictures of the cut. During the interim, contractors will negotiate with DRMO by bidding for the approximate 120,000 lb of metal. At the end of 90 days, the remains can be removed from AMARC premises.

This crane will be used to eliminate the B-52s in accordance with START. The vehicle weighs 140 tons and will free-fall a 13,000 lb guillotine blade 60-65 ft, severing the wings at the fuselage, the fuselage at the center wing box, and the aft (47) section aft of the aft main fuel cell.

▼ B-52G 59-2587, otherwise known as 'Stratofortress Rex', is being cut into seven foot sections to expedite the removal from AMARC prior to the treaty being ratified. The 13,000 lb guillotine is used to cut the aircraft. The initial cut occurred on 25 Mar. 92.

▲ The guillotine bearing the colors of the Aerospace Maintenance and Regeneration Center falls on B-52E 57-0121 after more than twenty-three years in storage. On 7 Jan. 70-0121 arrived at AMARC from the 96th Bomb Wing, Dyess AFB, TX, with a total of 5,595.5 flight hours. On 17 Aug. 93-0121 was the first B-52 to be cut in accordance with the requirements of START. Although the treaty ratification had not been signed, AMARC was authorized to start the cut of the first 100 B-52s of the 365 that are included in START.

▼ Once the mighty deterrent of the Cold War, this scrap heap is all that remains of the B-52E after it was cut into seven foot sections by the 13,000 lb guillotine blade. Approximately 120,000 lb of scrap metal is all that remains to be picked up by the contractor and melted down into aluminum ingots.

▲ Aerial view of a B-52 fuselage cut in segments.

▶ What was once the biggest deterrent to the Cold War is now a stack of shiny aluminum ingots.

▼ The chopped remains of B-52C 53-0405.

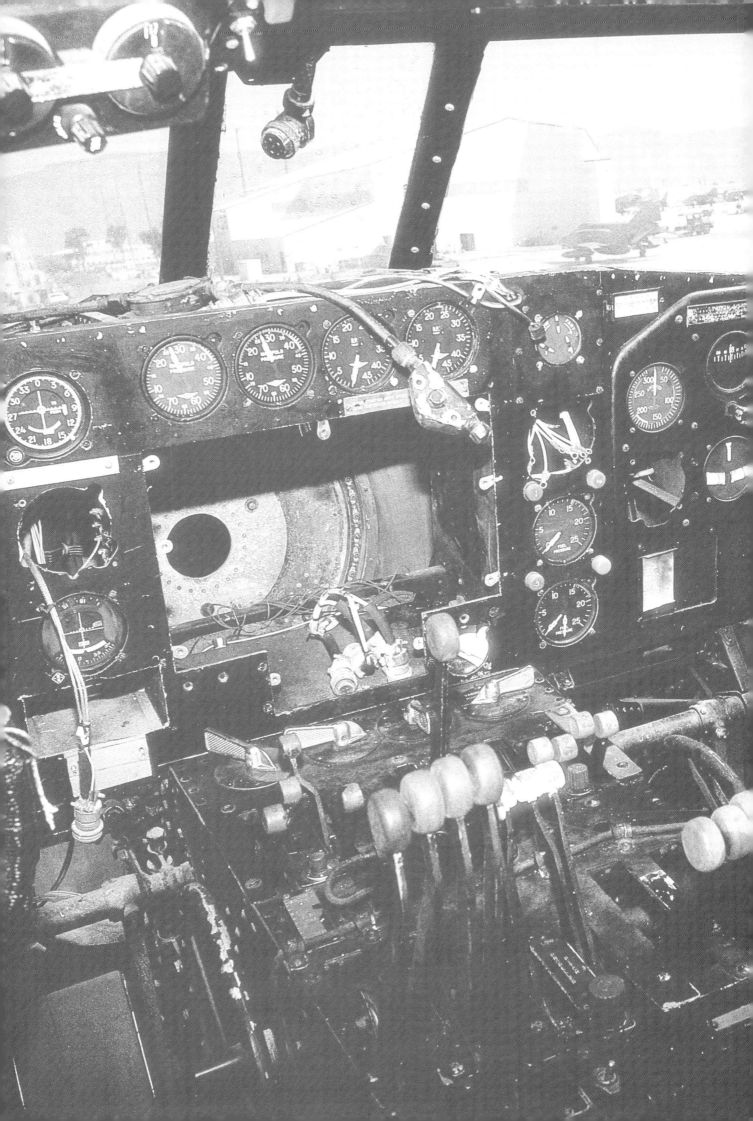

V
STORED AIRCRAFT
RETURNING
TO FLYING STATUS

▲ F-100F 56-3922 is another to deploy as a tow target aircraft for the Army. A total of three F-100Fs were deployed for the Army tow target program.

▼ This F-4E, formerly of Clark AFB, PI is being prepared as a prototype drone that will be a follow-on to the F-106 Drone Program. Eight F-4s were sent to Mojave to Tracor Flight Systems who will prepare the F-4s as remote controlled, ground operated air-to-air simulators (Drones). The F-4E/G/RF will enter the Program in the 1994/95 timeframe.

▲ Running the main landing gear of the Boeing 307 up and down can be frustrating and tedious. Here the landing gear are up and locked; however, the left gear would not come down and extensive maintenance was required to lower it. Further investigation revealed the landing gear motor had burned out and needed replacement.

▼ Such a beautiful sight! All four engines turning, No. 4 spitting a little, starving for more fuel, Nos 1 and 2 turning ever so smoothly. Quite an accomplishment after twenty years of lingering as a static display; Einer Moen at the throttles with Skip Wells on the headset, reminiscing as they listen to the purring of those engines.

This Boeing 307 cockpit controlled the four Pratt & Whitney 1820-47 engines for a total of 20,526 flight hours, flying to Mexico City from Los Angeles. It made daily round trips from New York to Bermuda, operated in South America during Word War II, and chauffeured the President of Haiti around as his Air Force One. These throttles were activated many times in 1992 as the Boeing Team was preparing the aircraft for flight after twenty years on display.

F-106A 59-0043, 'The Spirit of Atlantic City', was operated by the 177th FIS, NJ Air National Guard, prior to being stored at AMARC. This unique aircraft established a high speed record of 1525.5 miles per hour on 15 Dec. 59. The nose identifies all the F-106 units that operated as Air Defense Command units. This aircraft departed AMARC on 16 Dec. 92 and flew to AEL Corp., East Alton, IL to be modified as a remote controlled, ground operated air-to-air combat simulator (Drone). The airctaft was later returned to AMARC for use as a Museum static display.

This P-2H is a good example of what happens to an aircraft that has been declared excess to the Navy inventory. Once the aircraft is stricken it can become an asset to the Navy Museum to be used as trading material for something of commensurate value. This P-2H was traded and converted to a fire bomber, dropping fire retardant on forest fires.

▲ This OV-10 Bronco, after a brief stay at AMARC, was transferred to the Bureau of Land Management (BLM) where it is currently used by the agency as a lead airplane for fire fighting.

▼ This O-2A, a Vietnam veteran, left AMARC to be entered on the civil register as a result of an Air Force Museum trade.

This C-7A Caribou was one of five that departed AMARC as Air Force Museum trades and were flown to Mozambique, Africa, flying food to the outback country of Africa..

In September 1992, this C-121C 54-0157, after being towed from AMARC to the Pima Air and Space Museum, was being readied by the Sydney based Historic Aviation Restoration Society (HARS) Group for a flight to Australia. 54-0157 had been in storage at AMARC since July 1975.

The YC-15 returning from its final test flight after being in storage for eighteen years. The aircraft was delivered to Long Beach, CA, in May 1997.

INDEX OF AIRCRAFT TYPES